Keys To The Kingdom

by

Tosha Meredith

Keys To The Kingdom

Published in the United States of America by
The Dr. Tosha Meredith Foundation.
www.toshameredith.com

All rights reserved. No part of this publication may
be reproduced, distributed, or transmitted in any
form or by any means, including photocopying,
recording, or other electronic or mechanical
methods, without the prior written permission of
the publisher, except in the case of brief quotations embodied in critical reviews and certain
other noncommercial uses permitted by copyright
law. For permission requests, email the publisher,
addressed "Attention: Permissions Coordinator" in
the subject line to the address below.

The Dr. Tosha Meredith Foundation

info@toshameredith.com

www.toshameredith.com

Ordering Information:

Quantity Sales: Special discounts are available on quantity purchases by corporations, associations, and others. For details, contact the publisher at the address above.

Orders by U.S. trade bookstores and wholesalers. Please contact The Dr. Tosha Meredith Foundation. Distribution: Tel: 678-467-7416 or visit www.toshameredith.com. Printed in the United States of America

ISBN: 978-0-9914259-2-1

First Edition

Unless marked otherwise, all Scripture quotations are from the New International Version (NIV) English Version Copyright © 1973, 1978, 1984 by International Bible Society. Used by Permission

Dedication

This book is dedicated to you and to everyone searching for the Keys to the Kingdom.

Table of Contents

Key One: Be Somebody 1

  Nobody To Somebody! 1

Be Somebody Exercise 7

Key Two: Be Audacious 9

  Ask With Courage! 9

Be Audacious Exercise 17

Key Three: Be Impartial 19

  Fava Aint Fair! 19

Be Impartial Exercise... 25

Key Four: Be Authentic 27

  Kingdom Business! 27

Be Authentic Exercise 33

Key Five: Forgive 36

Because He Forgave You 36

Forgive Exercise 41

Key Six: Be Responsible 44

Do Your Part 44

Be Responsible Exercise 51

Key Seven: Put Faith Into Action 54

The Deal! 54

Put Faith Into Action Exercise 58

Epilogue 61

Prologue

Matthew 6:33 reads, "But seek first his kingdom and his righteousness, and all these things will be given to you as well." Many people think there is some sort of secret to inheriting the Kingdom of God. I submit to you that it is simple yet perplexed. Simple in the sense that God gives us the exact formula that we need to inherit the Kingdom. However, inheriting the Kingdom is a bit perplexed because of the human factor. We, as human beings, place limitations on ourselves and we restrict our level of happiness. Once we figure out how to prevent ourselves from placing limitations on ourselves, we will find the solutions to inheriting the Kingdom of God.

In this simple guide, I discuss seven "Keys To The Kingdom." These keys are very simple and perhaps so easy that they are almost unbelievable. However, it is my opinion that observing and subsequently implementing these simple keys will guide you to a more abundant life; a life of love, happiness, and joy. My prayer is that you will find some sort of resolve in the following reading. I pray that you will find the secrets you've been yearning for, the ones that have lead you straight to this book. In the mean time, be blessed and go forth and prosper.

Blessings,

Dr. Tosha Meredith

Key One: Be Somebody

Nobody To Somebody!

One of the most important things you can learn to do is recognize yourself as a special person in the Kingdom of God. It is probably the greatest decision you will ever make. When we recognize our value and our purpose both spiritually and physically, we can then contribute to both the spiritual realm and the physical realm. Though daunting, it is possible and sometimes we actually go from being a "nobody" to a "somebody" and we may not even realize we are going through the transition until after we have come out as a "somebody."

Allow me to introduce you to Mary, the mother of Jesus and the cousin to Elizabeth, John the Baptist's mother. Luke 1: 46-47 reads, "My soul glorifies the Lord and my spirit rejoices in God my Savior." When Mary said the now somewhat famous quote, some would say that she was probably not very popular in her community. I'm sure she didn't realize at that time that she was carrying the son of the Most High, Jesus Christ. Though she didn't know this important fact, just as many of us don't know our purpose as we are transitioning from being a "nobody" (in our minds) to becoming a "somebody" in the Kingdom, we recognize that God is a keeper of His promises. He fulfills His word to those who are faithful.

As you analyze not only what it takes to inherit the Kingdom of God but also what it takes to go from a nobody to a somebody, there are a few questions you must ask yourself; such as, what have I done to fulfill God's promises? If your soul could sing (out loud) what would it say? What would it sing? How does your soul's inner being take you from "nobody" to somebody? What does that mean or look like to you? You will have an opportunity to analyze these questions in detail at the end of this chapter. The exercise will provide you with time to answer the questions and also observe your feelings while answering.

Going from a nobody to a somebody can be looked at in many ways. For the purposes of this discussion, I would like to draw a parallel between going from a nobody (unsaved) to a somebody (saved) person. How does one, in particular a Christian, go from being a nobody once he is saved (accepts Jesus Christ as his Lord and Savior). A more important question to ponder is perhaps, why it's important or relevant for a Christian to make this transition.

According to The Gospel of Luke, there are some key reasons a person should go from being a nobody (unsaved) to a somebody. Remember our key text in Luke 1 about Mary, Jesus' mother. It was absolutely necessary for her to go from being a nobody to a somebody because she was carrying the Child of the Most High. She was carrying the person (Spirit) that had come to save and change the world. So if it was important for Mary to make that transition, I imagine it's certain-

Tosha Meredith

ly important for other mere mortals to make the transition.

The reasons it is relevant to be somebody in order to inherit the Kingdom of God are so that we Glorify God in our transition, show others evidence of God's mercy, and to let people know that God fulfills His promises to us. Psalm 111 talks about exalting The Lord because He has been so mindful of our needs and He takes care of us. According to Luke 1 we should glorify The Lord because it is the right thing to do. The word glory means to bring "public praise, honor, and fame." When I think of glorifying God, I imagine honoring Him in the highest sense. Giving Him the highest praise. If I am to inherit all that God has for me, I most certainly am going to exalt His name every chance I get.

Secondly, we must constantly show others the goodness of God. It is one thing to glorify God but it's an entirely different story to show others the mercy God has shown us. What if we could show mercy to others in the same manner in which God shows mercy to us? Wouldn't that be a phenomenal thing? I think that is one of the most important aspects of our transition to becoming somebody. Revisiting the story about Mary and her transition to becoming somebody, she gave God the glory, honor, and praise in advance. She was committed to serving Him even before Jesus' birth. We should show that same passion during our transition. We want to be sure to show kindness and mercy to everyone we encounter. Doing this will ensure that we receive the promises of God.

Luke 1 mentions that God fulfilled His promise in the days before Christ. God promised Abraham that his offspring would rule over many nations and God fulfilled His promises several generations later. The transition to becoming somebody requires us to acknowledge God's promises and to also be open to knowing that God will fulfill his promises. Trusting in God often times requires faith in knowing the possibilities. Once we decide to go from nobody to somebody, we have to demonstrate a great deal of faith knowing and

Tosha Meredith

believing that God will fulfill His promises. This, my friend, is a key to inheriting the Kingdom of God.

Going from nobody to somebody is a process that starts from birth. In spiritual reference, going from being unsaved to saved and walking under the covering of God is powerful! We should Glorify God every chance we get! And we should also acknowledge His mercies and greatness! People will naturally see how we went from nobody to somebody (and not from material perspective but a spiritual perspective!)

Be Somebody Exercise

"My soul glorifies the Lord and my spirit rejoices in God my Savior." Luke 1:46-47

1.   Are you somebody?

_____

_____

_____

_____

_____

2.   How do you know you are/are not some-body?

_____

_____

_____

_____

_____

Tosha Meredith

3.   What are you doing to enhance your life?

_____

_____

_____

_____

_____

4.   Do your physical and spiritual lives mirror one another?

_____

_____

_____

_____

_____

5.   What steps can you take to remain/ become somebody TODAY?

_____

_____

_____

_____

_____

Key Two: Be Audacious

Ask With Courage!

When we go to God with an audacious spirit and trust and believe that God is going to grant our requests, I believe that we can rest assured that our requests will be granted because that's how awesome our God is. Audacity has two distinct meanings. The first meaning is to make a bold or courageous request (Positive). The second meaning is to ask with nerve or arrogance (Negative, considering the situation). In 1 Kings 3 we find that Solomon asked with both courage and arrogance. Solomon asked for "wisdom" so he could lead Gods people (courage). However, Solomon also asked in somewhat arrogance because he was known to have worshiped in shrines and high places while making burnt offerings, but not to God.

I don't know about you, but I have been in a space where I've made requests known to God knowing He was the ONLY source for me accomplishing it! I have also made requests to God knowing that I was in a sinful state and that it was downright arrogant of me to ask God to bring me out of something I KNOW I got myself into! So like Solomon, we ask with an audacious spirit; having both courage and arrogance at the same time. I would like to focus on the former, courage, relative to asking with audacity in this context!

Some Questions to Ponder:

1. What are you believing God for that you have not yet asked for?

2. When was the last time you went boldly to the throne of God?

3. Who is it that you need to leave in the past so that your future victory can manifest itself?

4. When asking God to help you leave something or someone in the past; when asking God to give you that "thing" you've been waiting for; when asking God to grant you that clean bill of

Get In The Flow

health, or to get those bills paid, or to bless you with a level of anointing so strong and powerful that when you walk in the room, you flow with the Spirit of the Living God and the ENTIRE room elevates to a level of peace that surpasses all understanding...when asking God those things do you ask with an audacious spirit?

5. Why then should we make these requests, as Solomon did, with an audacious or courageous spirit?

God Already Knows Your Request!

Looking at the text we find that Solomon was worshiping shrines in high places. Don't you know that God already knew what Solomon was doing! God already knew every burnt offering Solomon made in those shrines! Perhaps God wanted to give Solomon a way out, a choice to a better life.

Have you ever had a person ask you a loaded question? I mean, a question where you know that they already knew the answer or at least knew the answer they were looking for? Well, I believe that God is a "loaded" God! God knows what we are going to do before we even do it. God knows our end before we even begin!

A few weeks ago at our ministers meeting Pastor P mentioned that he knows what our (the ministers) response is likely to be in most situations. Pastor mentioned that he intently "learns" each one of his ministers so that he can know and understand their personality. God is just like that! God knows each one of us and He knows our personality. He knew us before he formed us and knew every move we would make and when we would make it. Because God knows this, I believe we can boldly ask our requests because God already knows what our action will be prior to His answer. All He wants us to do is make the decision.

Your Destiny Depends on It!

If you haven't already done so, please take some time to read the entire chapter on this phase of Solomon's life. You will find that his riches and knowledge were greater that any man that lived then and likely greater that any man that

Get In The Flow 13

has lived to this day. Solomon's destiny and assignment depended on the audacious request he made to God! His past (negative) life did not predict his future (positive) life or his destiny with God. I would argue that Solomon's bold requests thrust him into not only his destiny, but, ultimately, into his Kingdom assignment.

Have you ever had an aha moment when you realized that one phase of your life was over and a new phase was beginning?

I'm reminded of the story of then Senator Barrack Obama back in 2008 when he ran for the President of the United States. Senator Obama's campaign slogan was "Yes we can!" There were billboards, bumper stickers and t-shirts with "Yes We Can!" written all over them. Once President Obama won the office the slogan quickly became "Yes We Did" and you began to see that all over the United States. But during President Obama's first term there were of course ups and downs and I imagine there were times in his mind where his slogan was, "Can I do this?" Well, it was about

14 Tosha Meredith

2010 when the debate on healthcare began to really take its course. President Obama demonstrated such a level of courage and resiliency that you could almost look into his eyes and know that he realized his life and decisions would have a direct impact on the lives of many others.

I believe it was then that President Obama realized that his audacious spirit back in 2008 and that slogan of "Yes We Can" determined not only the destiny of his family, but the destiny and lives of everyone living in the United States. I believe, like Solomon, President Obama realized that his Kingdom assignment (not his destiny) was playing out before his very eyes...and all because he had the courage and the audacity to "ask." He demonstrated the courage and audacity to do something that had never been done before in the history of America. When you get to the point that Solomon and President Obama were at...when you get to the point of asking God the bold questions...when you realize that your Kingdom assignment is greater than anything that could ever creep up from your past, then and only then will you be able to move forward in your destiny. That Kingdom movement will determine the livelihood of your future. Having an audacious spirit is important...

Your Future is Brighter Than Your Past!

Solomon was known as the child who was born from an affair. He was known to worship in shrines and he was somewhat of a lady's man, for a lack of better words. However, I believe that God knew when he told Solomon to ask for whatever it was that he wanted, God knew that Solomon's life would change based on his request.

There are things in our life that we should be doing. There are people in our life that we need to let go of. Quite frankly, there are some decisions that need to be made in this very moment because your future depends on it and other's souls depend on it. God knows the decision you are contemplating and God already knows the request you have of him. Like he did with Solomon,

God is going to grant your requests if you ask with an audacious spirit, with the courage of Daniel.

Your future depends on your request and your future is brighter than anything that you've ever done. Won't you be like Solomon, ask for the wisdom you need to have a better future, to live a Kingdom centered life, to be thrust into your destiny. Your future is brighter than your past! Going to God with an audacious spirit requires faith and perseverance in knowing and believing in whom you trust. Know that God has your back and that The Lord already knows your requests. Believe that your audacious request is directly tied to your destiny and your purpose in life. Your boldness in your request may be the determining factor in you beginning or continuing to live out your purpose and assignment in this life. Be Bold! Be Audacious! Be Persistent and ask God for the desires of your heart and watch God Move!

Be Audacious Exercise

"…ask for whatever it is you want…" 1 Kings 3:5b

6.   Are you an audacious person?

_____

_____

_____

_____

_____

7.   What does audacity mean to you?

_____

_____

_____

_____

_____

18 Tosha Meredith

8. What does courage mean to you?

_____

_____

_____

_____

_____

9. What should you be asking for NOW that you have held off on?

_____

_____

_____

_____

_____

10. What steps can you take to begin/continue to live an audacious life?

_____

_____

_____

_____

_____

Key Three: Be Impartial

Fava Aint Fair!

Looking at James 1 and 2 we find that the bible speaks against showing partiality toward individuals. It is important for us to be impartial if we want to gain the keys to the Kingdom! James 1:1 reads, "My brothers and sisters, believers in our glorious Lord Jesus Christ must not show favoritism." Favoritism is somewhat of a natural behavior. We show favoritism to those we love and care for. However, it is important for us to not only show kindness to those we love and care for, but also to those we may not know; a random stranger on the street or a beggar in the ally, or perhaps the witnesses who randomly knock on our door on Saturday mornings. It is hard to acknowledge, but loving as God does means consciously reaching out to those who are unlike us in various ways.

20   Tosha Meredith

If one professes to be a Christian and follow the ways of Jesus Christ, it is even more important not to show partiality. Basically, favoritism and Christianity are incompatible. They do not mesh well together and they are not one in the same. There are four points to consider relative to why favoritism and Christianity are incompatible, according to the bible, that is.

First and foremost, the two are incompatible because the bible clearly speaks against favoritism. We find in Romans that we are to love our neighbor as we love our self. We also find in the book of Acts that God doesn't show partiality towards believers. Subsequently, if God doesn't show partiality, who are we to show it? When I was a child growing up, there were five of us. I had one brother that I grew up with and three other cousins. I was the second to the youngest of the five and the youngest between my brother and I. We didn't get very many spankings as children (in hindsight, that is). However, often times when we did get spankings EVERYBODY

Get In The Flow 21

got one! And I do mean EVERBODY!!! If one child caused trouble, all the children paid for it. I wouldn't change it for the world though, because it showed that our parents or family unit did not show favoritism, no matter the circumstance. Just as God doesn't show favoritism, we should not either.

The second point demonstrating the incompatibility between favoritism and Christianity is that when one shows partiality, they cast judgment on another; something that is forbidden as well. What do I mean by this? Well, when we look at the Bible, specifically James 2, we find the author says that if one shows partiality to a rich person or person dressed in fine clothes and pays no attention to the poor person, or poorly dressed person, judgment occurs. For example, the scripture says, "Suppose a man comes into your meeting wearing a gold ring and fine clothes, and a poor man in filthy old clothes also comes in. If you show special attention to the man wearing fine clothes and say, "Here's a good seat for you,"

22 Tosha Meredith

but say to the poor man, "You stand there " or "Sit on the floor by my feet," have you not discriminated among yourselves and become judges with evil thoughts? (James 2:2-4, NIV)"

The third point in looking at the incompatibility between favoritism and Christianity is the importance of practicing the Golden Rule. If we treat others the way we want to be treated, will we not be impartial to everyone? I submit that we will practice and exemplify impartiality. Here's why: when we look at what's called transformational valuation we find that the experiences that we have had in the past, help us with our current experiences. Transformational valuation means that we transform our experiences of favoritism or discrimination into valuation in another. Basically, we find the highest good in another person.

Allow me to illustrate. In about 2007 I began attending a church that's considered to be an "Affirming" or "Love and Acceptance Church." Basically, what this is supposed to mean, is that everyone is welcomed, straight and gay, black

Get In The Flow

and white, etc. Well, I noticed after attending the church for a few years that the experiences I'd felt when I attended traditional churches in the past, such as being made to feel like an outcast or that I didn't belong in a Christian church, were the very things that were done to the "traditional" people who came to the non-traditional church. To put it plainly, I witnessed straight people being made to feel uncomfortable in the church that is traditionally attended by gay people. It was the craziest things I'd ever witnessed. However, because of the way I was treated (my experiences) in the traditional church in the past, I was able to identify with this experience of discrimination and attempt to prevent it or at least bring it to the forefront at the affirming or love and acceptance church. Transformational valuation. I was able to take the experiences of my past, apply them to my present, and hopefully make a change for the better in the future. Again, the golden rule of treating others the way we want to be treated. It seems like a basic principle and it really is, however, it's not always practiced like it should be.

The final point in looking at how favoritism and Christianity are incompatible is the basic fact that showing favoritism is a sin. In the Bible, James 2:9 reads. "But if you show favoritism, you sin and are convicted by the law as law breakers." Many people look at some sin as being greater that other sin. However, sin is sin, in my humble opinion. Here we see that if we profess to be Christians and we show favoritism, or impartiality, towards an individual or certain group of people, we are sinning at the very foundational level of Christianity. It really is that simple. The bottom line is that if we want to inherit the keys to the Kingdom, we have to be impartial, non-judgmental, and merciful. "We ask God for mercy that he strengthens us to overcome the patterns of this world by which we ignore members of our family, our brothers and our sisters. Let us love one another as God has loved us."

Be Impartial Exercise

"My brothers and sisters, believers in our glorious Lord Jesus Christ must not show favoritism." James 1:1

11.   Do you show favoritism in your personal or spiritual life?

_____

_____

_____

_____

_____

12.   If so, to whom do you show favoritism?

_____

_____

_____

_____

_____

Is favoritism fair to you?

_____

_____

_____

_____

_____

13.　How can you be more impartial and less judgmental?

_____

_____

_____

_____

_____

14.　What steps can you take to be more impartial toward individuals?

_____

_____

_____

_____

_____

Key Four: Be Authentic

Kingdom Business!

Psalm 139: 14-16 reads, "I praise you because I am fearfully and wonderfully made; your works are wonderful, I know that full well. My frame was not hidden from you when I was made in the secret place, when I was woven together in the depths of the earth. Your eyes saw my unformed body; all the days ordained for me were written in your book before one of them came to be." I've spent a lot of time trying to figure out who I am and whose I am. It wasn't until I realized that I am "fearfully and wonderfully" made in God's image that I began to live my authentic life. Many people talk about being and living authentically but I wonder if most are able to really do it.

Living an authentic life can sometimes be challenging for everyone involved. Authenticity requires honesty and transparency. As I write this chapter my ability to live authentically is being challenged. Why write about it? Because transparency is a part of authenticity. Being transparent allows the environment for living an open and honest life.

This morning's church service was one of the most uncomfortable services I've ever attended. My pastor preached about being inline with and committed to the vision of the (current) church I attend. What made me the most uncomfortable was the way in which the message was delivered. It seemed that the pastor was insinuating that if one was not in line with the vision of the church then he or she was not in line with the process (will) of God, that not being in line with the vision of the church could somehow throw one off track of their divine purpose.

You may ask why I am writing about this in the chapter on being and living an authentic life. Well, in my opinion, sometimes living an authentic life may "appear" to others as being out of the will of God or out of line with the vision of certain people.

As I mentioned at the beginning of this chapter, living authentically requires honesty, loyalty, and transparency. Living an honest life requires one to be open and sincere about the path God has you on. For example, I now know that I have an Apostolic call on my life and that I am to contribute to the Kingdom God through aiding ministries around the world. An apostle by definition is someone who plants churches, generally speaking.

I have to be honest with myself and know that my call is not to join and remain at any one church. In fact, I believe my call is to have what I call a "church without walls," a church without all the politics and issues that come a long with having a physical building, if you will. Being open and honest about that allows me to realize that when it comes to supporting others visions, if they limit the visions God has placed in my life, then I am not living in authenticity; I am not living honestly. So looking at the example of the pastor and his position on wanting his members to follow his vision and his vision only or they will be out of alignment with the church tells me that in order to live authentically and be true and honest with this particular church, it is likely in my best interest to find another church to rest my soul for a while, a church where my spiritual gifts can be utilized while carrying out the visions God has given me and also carrying out the vision of the church that I'd be in fellowship with.

Authenticity also requires doing the right thing even when it doesn't feel good. I didn't feel "good" sitting in church today listening to what I compare to a slave mentality or oppression-like perspective on the church. It saddens me to know that many churches are still living in and practicing slavery-day theology and leadership (or the lack thereof). I recently said on one of my radio show broadcasts that many churches are places that should be safe havens for individuals to find freedom. However, many churches, the very place where people should be able to go and find freedom, have become beating grounds, and places where

Get In The Flow 31

oppressed individuals take liberty in oppressing members and leaders within the church.

Living authentically requires individuals to stand and speak up for what and who they believe regardless of whether they will be judged about it or not. Living authentically requires individuals to stand up to pastors and leaders who shun them when they are no longer in line with "the vision" of their organization. Living authentically requires walking away when it feels good and even when it doesn't feel good. Living authentically is knowing when it's time to go and when it's time to push the reset button.

Pushing the reset button allows you to move on to your God-given destiny and purpose. Jeremiah 29:11 reads, "For I know the plans I have for you," declares the Lord, "plans to prosper you and not to harm you, plans to give you hope and a future." When you live an authentic life, you clear your pathway for God's plans to come into alignment with the universe. You create the environment and the conditions you want to manifest in your life. You create and control the Keys to the Kingdom.

Be Authentic Exercise

"I praise you because I am fearfully and wonderfully made; your works are wonderful, I know that full well. My frame was not hidden from you when I was made in the secret place, when I was woven together in the depths of the earth. Your eyes saw my unformed body; all the days ordained for me were written in your book before one of them came to be." Psalms 39-14-16

15. In what areas of your life do you live authentically?

_____

_____

_____

_____

_____

16. In what areas of your life do you need to increase your authenticity?

_____

_____

_____

_____

_____

17. What does authenticity look like or mean to you?

_____

_____

_____

_____

_____

18. Does your life mirror that of an authentic lifestyle?

_____

_____

_____

Get In The Flow

19. What steps can you take to begin to live a more authentic life TODAY?

Key Five: Forgive

Because He Forgave You

Many years ago, I began to read the scripture about forgiveness in an effort to forgive someone who hurt me, probably, the most I've ever been hurt before. I remember reading Matthew 6:14 over and over, day after day, with no change in feeling, no light bulb moment, no dismissal of the hurt I'd felt for years and years. It wasn't until I attended a church service one morning and the Bishop preached about "forgiving my father." Now, it wasn't my father who I was upset with; or so I didn't think. However, it was something in that sermon that made me realize the importance of unequivocally forgiving the person whom I felt had offended me.

Matthew 6: 14-15 reads, "For if you forgive men their trespasses, your heavenly Father will also forgive you. But if you do not forgive men

Get In The Flow 37

their trespasses, neither will your Father forgive your trespasses." The part that eventually got to me was that if I didn't forgive I wasn't going to be forgiven by God! That is no easy pill to swallow! And the journey of forgiveness began for me personally.

In order to inherit the keys to the Kingdom you must forgive yourself and you must forgive others who have wronged you. One of the most difficult things to do is to ask God for forgiveness (and really mean it). God says that all of our sins are forgiven, so why it is so hard to ask Him to forgive us? I believe it's because it's really hard to forgive ourselves. When we harm ourselves or do things that cause us pain, it can be very difficult to not only get over the pain but to also forgive ourselves and forget the pain.

I remember a comment I made to my mother when I was in high school. It was an inappropriate comment, certainly for a 16 year old. Really, it was inappropriate for a daughter (or son for that matter) of any age. It was very hurtful (or so I thought) to my mom and I didn't think before I spoke. However, once the words went forth in the atmosphere, it was too late to take them back. I never forgot those words and I'd always wondered if my mom had forgiven me. Well, a few years back I struck up the nerves to ask my mom about the incident and to seek her forgiveness. Needless to say, she had forgiven me long ago and honestly probably had not given the situation much thought since it happened. I, on the other end, never forgave myself about it. In fact, it ate me up for a long time. I always wanted to take the words back but couldn't.

After apologizing to my mom about the situation, I finally forgave myself, however I must admit the words are still fresh in my mind. Harboring negative feelings and not forgiving myself for all those years not only hurt me, but also it may have hurt some of the individuals around me. Carrying negative feelings and failing to forgive yourself can be an internal nightmare that never ends. It never ends, that is, until you finally forgive yourself. It is important to realize that forgiving oneself is just as important as asking someone else for forgiveness. In fact, it may be even more important because we carry the guilt and burden of the situation into other relationships long after the incident has occurred. The key is realizing that when God says we are forgiven, we are forgiven. All we have to do is ask.

The second component of forgiveness is having the ability to forgive others. When I was a little girl, probably around four years old, my stepfather sexually molested me. He molested me until I was about 10 years old. It's unfortunate but I didn't forgive him until very recently. In fact I can remember the day I forgave him. It was about 7 years ago after the sermon I heard my Bishop preach about forgiving our fathers. Though it took me what seemed like a lifetime to muster up the courage to forgive my stepfather, I finally did. And when I did, I must say it was the most freeing thing I had ever done. I felt like a million dollars!

I'd spent the preceding 10 years reading the scripture, Matthew 6:14 on an almost daily basis. I wanted to forgive but I really didn't know how to do it or what to say. I wanted to be forgiven by God for any times I'd required or requested forgiveness. But more than that, I wanted to get to the point where I was truly in a place where I could not only forgive the man who took my innocence away at such an early age, but also to the point where I loved him totally, completely, and unconditionally. And I did. I forgave him and never looked back. My life has been so much richer and lighter since that day. I can rest knowing that I've forgiven my stepfather and God has forgiven me for any ill-doings I've ever done. That, my friends, is certainly a key to the Kingdom, experiencing the level of freedom that comes with forgiveness and unconditional love after that forgiveness.

Forgive Exercise

"For if you forgive men their trespasses, your heavenly Father will also forgive you. But if you do not forgive men their trespasses, neither will your Father forgive your trespasses." Matthew 6: 14-15

20. In what areas of your life do you have complete forgiveness?

_____

_____

_____

_____

_____

21. In what areas of your life do you need to increase your forgiveness?

_____

_____

_____

_____

_____

22.   Do you have people you need to forgive? If so, who are they? Identify them here:

_____

_____

_____

_____

_____

23.   Does your forgiveness depend on another person? If so, who?

_____

_____

_____

_____

_____

Get In The Flow 43

24. What steps can you take to get your begin to forgive TODAY?

_____

_____

_____

_____

_____

Key Six: Be Responsible

Do Your Part

Each one of these keys is important but I would have to say that being responsible and doing your part is one of the most significant parts of inheriting the keys to the Kingdom. It is so crucial for us to take the necessary steps to getting what we want in life, to helping others in their quest of this thing called life. Looking at responsibility from a biblical perspective we can observe Abraham and his level of responsibility or commitment to God.

In Genesis 17:1 we find, "When Abram was ninety-nine years old, the Lord appeared to him and said, 'I am God Almighty; walk before me faithfully and be blameless. Then I will make my covenant between me and you and will greatly increase your numbers'." God gave specific instructions on what Abraham needed to do to receive the promises of God. It was then Abra-

Get In The Flow

ham's responsibility to carry out the dream, to be responsible for his destiny and purpose in life. In fact, it wasn't only his life he would be responsible for, but the lives of many generations to come.

The key in looking at responsibility is knowing that nothing is too hard for our God, subsequently; there is nothing too hard for us as believers. We must take the necessary actions for carrying out our dreams just as Abraham was instructed to do and subsequently did. We can look at Isaiah 51 for specific instructions on what we need to do in doing "our part" in gaining the keys to the Kingdom. The first thing we must do is listen to God's voice; listen to our voice. We must do our part in fulfilling the covenant so that God's promises come to fruition.

Isaiah 51:1 reads, "Listen to me, you who pursue righteousness and who seek the Lord. Look to the rock from which you were cut and to the quarry from which you were hewn." Listening to God is so important; in fact it may be the most important part of being responsible. Being responsible means being obedient to yourself, to the God in you; listening to the voice of God in you. Knowing "how" to hear Gods voice is important because you must know how to identify Gods voice if you are to listen to Gods voice. Once you learn that the still, quiet voice that you hear when you are making decisions, or when you know you are supposed to go in the opposite direction of where you are doing, that's the God in you. That's the voice of God you must learn to listen to in order to inherit the keys to the Kingdom. Listening to the voice of God requires that you become vulnerable not only to yourself but also to those around you.

Vulnerability is something that not many people are willing to accept and experience. But when you can become vulnerable to God, to yourself, and to those around you, you can create the type of environment you want and need to get ahead in life. You created the environment necessary for physical and spiritual growth. Vulnerability is defined as, "susceptibility to physical or

Get In The Flow

47

emotional attack or harm." This means that you have to be willing to open yourself up to "attack or harm." This means you have to be willing and ready for the spiritual battles that may come as a result of opening yourself up. Realize that the more vulnerable you become, the more that God can and will protect you. Vulnerability isn't a liability; it is an asset if used properly.

We must realize that when we become vulnerable, we change. We change internally and externally. We don't look the same. We don't think the same. Nor do we act the same. And that's a good, no, great, thing! It is important for us to recognize and appreciate how important it is to not only change but to sometimes change your name! Yes! Change your name. What do I mean by this?   When I was much younger, I hung out in strip clubs and dance clubs. I was known as Durrty Redd to many of the strippers. Likely, if I were to see someone today on the street that I knew from the strip club or the dance club, they would say, 'Hey Redd! Sup!" This might sound

48   Tosha Meredith

funny but I'm going somewhere with it.☐ Though
that was my nickname at the time, or back in the
day as we say, that's no longer who I am. Now, I
am "Dr. Meredith." Not only in title, but also in
stature and in physical and spiritual meanings. I
am no longer that person. I had to change. I mean
literally change my name as I escaped the streets
and transitioned into the person God has called
and is calling me to be. Now, the people I meet
call me "Dr. Meredith."

It took me a long time to get used to this name
and it was in fact my mother who suggested that I
start using my title a few years back. I didn't
understand it at the time but I certainly understand it now. Changing ones name is essential.
It's crucial. It's a must. Genesis 17:5 reads, "No
longer will you be called Abram; your name will be
Abraham, for I have made you a father of many
nations." So if God deemed it so important to
change names, that he himself changed the name
of a man as great as Abraham, don't you think it's
important, also then, for you and I to change our

names; to create the atmosphere that we now want to walk in; to leave the past behind us and embrace the future with a new, more reflective name? I think so and subsequently have changed my name to reflect not only my now, but my future! Finally, if you want to be responsible, it is imperative that you keep the faith. Not only must you have faith, but you must keep the faith. Recognizing your potential and purpose is one thing but to excel to an entirely different level of thinking and action is another. If you want to demonstrate responsibility, one of the greatest things you can do is to keep your faith intact. From a biblical perspective, having and maintained faith is the cornerstone of the Christian belief system. I mean, it's obvious to me because the religion in and of itself requires one to have faith that Jesus died for our sins and that He is one day coming back for us. That's a lot of faith! Imagine the level of faith required to not only believe something like this but to also put that faith into action and apply the principles of this

Jesus Christ person or entity. The final chapter of this book will re-emphasize the importance of not only keeping the faith but maintaining faith and putting faith into action. Listening, allowing oneself to be vulnerable, and changing our name are all keys to being responsible and inheriting the kingdom of God. Faith in action is the final key and it is a must have if YOU want to inherit the keys to the Kingdom.

Be Responsible Exercise

"When Abram was ninety-nine years old, the Lord appeared to him and said, "I am God Almighty; walk before me faithfully and be blameless. Then I will make my covenant between me and you and will greatly increase your numbers." Genesis 17:1

25.   In what areas of your life are you completely responsible?

_____

_____

_____

_____

_____

26.   In what areas of your life do you need to increase your level of responsibility?

_____

_____

27. Are you vulnerable to yourself, to God, to others?

28. Do you need to change your name to reflect your "now" or your "future" destiny?

Get In The Flow 53

29. What steps can you take to be more
     responsible TODAY?

_____

_____

_____

_____

_____

Key Seven: Put Faith Into Action

The Deal!

You know one of the things that puzzles me the most about some Christians is their ability to talk about faith yet they sometimes display a lack of faith when it comes to putting action behind the faith. What do I mean by this? Well, have you ever spoken to someone who professes to be a Christian and they also have been waiting for that "pie in the sky" or that "miracle pill?" I sure have met some people like that. I've met individuals who say that they trust God to "bring them through" a storm, yet they won't even get the umbrella out to prevent themselves from getting rained on. We have got to not only have unshakable faith, but we've also got to have unshakable action behind that faith.

James 2:26 reads, "As the body without the spirit is dead, so faith without deeds is dead." I interpret this particular scripture to mean that we can have faith, however, we've also got to work to make our dreams come true; those dreams that we have faith in. In order to put work behind our faith, I believe there are a few elements we must ponder: what we have faith in; where we draw our faith from; and how we keep our faith alive.

When looking at what we have faith in it is important to look at our circle of influence. The key things, people, and places that are a part of your circle of influence will determine in what things you have your faith. Does your circle of influences consist of church, leadership, family, friends, or associates? Do you take time to evaluate and nourish your friendships? Looking at your circle of influence will help you determine where your faith lies. Does your circle of influence encourage, uplift, and support you or does your circle of influence carry a negative and complaining spirit? Do your friends support your dream or do they negate your calling? Does your circle of influence require you to pour in to them or are they constantly taking away from you; draining your energy and spirit? Once you answer these questions, you will be able to determine what you have faith in. This determination will help you assess where you draw your faith.

I personally am a Christian and it is very important for me to meditate and pray on a consistent basis. This is where I draw my faith. God is my source and my supply and I must stay in constant contact with Him in order to draw strength and courage. God helps me evaluate who to put my trust and faith in and when and where to put my action into faith. Putting God first allows me to go forth with the necessary energy to overcome challenges and obstacles that may attempt to sabotage my dreams and aspirations. God, being the source that He is, allows me to ignite the necessary fuel for putting action behind the faith.

The final point, keeping faith alive is so important for putting action behind your faith. Praying without ceasing requires discipline and

Get In The Flow 57

energy. It requires that we put away certain time frames that are only for God, only for meditating and spending time alone in that sacred space. This time is so important for inheriting the keys to the Kingdom because without knowing the source of your soul, it is impossible to display faith, let alone put faith behind actions. We must be able to have faith, draw faith from our higher source, and keep our faith alive in order to put action behind that faith.

As I wrote in the first part of the "Get In The Flow" Series, having faith requires discipline and courage. Courage and integrity will help you to put action behind those words, thoughts, and dreams. Now, go forth and prosper.

Put Faith Into Action Exercise

"As the body without the spirit is dead, so faith without deeds is dead." James 2:26

30.   In what areas of your life do you have complete faith?

_____

_____

_____

_____

_____

31.   In what areas of your life do you need to increase your faith?

_____

_____

_____

_____

_____

Get In The Flow 59

32. In what areas of your life do you need to put your faith into action?

_____

_____

_____

_____

_____

33. Do you have enough faith to inherit the Keys to the Kingdom?

_____

_____

_____

_____

_____

34. What steps can you take to put your faith into action TODAY?

_____

_____

_____

Epilogue

Getting in the flow and inheriting the Kingdom has more to do with our faith and actions behind our faith, in my humble opinion. Learning to identify and implement the keys to the Kingdom will help us live a more abundant and responsible life. Being courageous, audacious, responsible, forgiving, loving, and faithful are all important elements to inheriting the keys to the Kingdom of God and living a more copious life. Knowing how to identify and implement these principles is key to your success. Not only is identifying the keys important, but it is also important to be sure to put action behind your faith. That is the final and perhaps most important key to the Kingdom of God.

About the Author

Lieutenant Colonel (Ret.) Meredith is a graduate of the University of Phoenix where she received her Doctor of Business Administration degree in 2007. She received her Master of Business Administration degree from the University of Wisconsin-Milwaukee in 1996. Lt Col (R) Meredith also earned a Master of Military Operational Art and Science at the Air Command and Staff College in 2009. In 2013 Lt Col (R) Meredith received a Master of Arts Education specializing in Adult Education and Training from the University of

Phoenix. Her Bachelor of Science comes from Marian University of Fond Du Lac, Wisconsin.

Lt Col (R) Meredith was most recently a Research Assistant for the Center for Strategy and Technology at Air University; she was also a college professor for the University of Phoenix, School of Business Administration for over seven years.

Dr. Meredith takes great pride in offering affordable housing for low-to-moderate income citizens. Dr. Meredith is also the owner of Transformational Management Services, Inc, a management consulting firm. The firm specializes in providing Financial Literacy Training for low-to moderate income citizens and attempts to "change the economy one mind at a time."

Dr. Meredith has over 25 years of experience managing multi-million dollar budgets. She is an active member and Elder at Victory In Christ United Fellowship of Churches. Dr. Meredith founded The Dr. Tosha Meredith Foundation in 2012 in which she does charity work and travels internationally doing mission work. Dr. Meredith is a sought after Motivational Speaker. Dr. Meredith delivered the keynote address at Marian University's Commencement Ceremony in May 2014. The Live, Love, Laugh! Radio Broadcast is the ultimate platform where Dr. Meredith conducts motivational speaking, as she is the host of the weekly talk shows "Live, Love, Laugh," "Monday Morning Glory," and "Tuesday Talk With Dr. Meredith."

Dr. Meredith is the author of the self-published book, "Get In The Flow – 7 Principles on Becoming a Wealthy Christian." She is also the author of the upcoming memoir, "Didn't Ask, Didn't Tell – A Story of Meritorious Service.

Printed in the USA
CPSIA information can be obtained
at www.ICGtesting.com
LVHW022302020224
770781LV00003B/456